A gift of Healing

To..

From..

FULL CIRCLE

Other **FULL CIRCLE** Books in this series

- Quotations for HAPPINESS
- Quotations for PEACE
- Quotations for LOVE
- Quotations for SUCCESS
- Quotations for HOPE
- Quotations for COMFORT
- Quotations for FRIENDSHIP
- Quotations for HEALING

FULL CIRCLE *Quotations* *for* *Healing*

Compiled by
Simran Singh

FULL CIRCLE

Full Circle Quotations for HEALING

Complied by Simran Singh

First Paperback Edition, 2003
First Reprint: 2003
Second Reprint: 2004
Third Reprint: 2006
Fourth Reprint: 2007
Fifth Reprint: 2013
Sixth Reprint: 2019

ISBN 13: 978-81-7621-143-7

Published by **FULL CIRCLE PUBLISHING**
J-40, Jorbagh Lane, New Delhi-110003
Tel: +011-24621011
E-mail: contact@fullcirclebooks.in • *www.*fullcirclebooks.in

Design & Layout : *SCANSET*
J-40, Jorbagh Lane, New Delhi-110003

Printed at Yash Printographics, C-37, Sector-58, Noida-201301 U.P.

PRINTED IN INDIA

Healing

It would be very wise to listen to yourself very carefully. You never know when you will say exactly what you need to hear.

Iyanla Vanzant

Everything is contained sounds — the past, the present, and the future. The person who does not know how to listen will never hear the advice that life offers us all the time.

And only the person who listens to the sounds of the moment is able to make the right decisions.

Paulo Coelho

In order to truly listen we have to truly empty ourselves, even of our distaste for expressions of pain and suffering.

M. Scott Peck

Listening is a wonderful gift we can choose to open each day.

Anon

Your doubts will never be totally destroyed until perception has gone beyond mere phenomenality, and such perception is not a matter of will but of Grace.

R. S. Balasekar

Since we cannot see reality, let us change the eyes which see reality.

Nikos Kazantzakis

Gratitude is the heart's memory.

A French proverb

I can live two months on a compliment.

Mark Twain

By appreciating we make excellence in others our own property.

Voltaire

Brains, like hearts,
go where they are
appreciated.

Robert McNamara

Every word that is not bathed in thought is a stone tossed in our path.

Rudolph Steiner

I think, therefore
I am.

René Descartes

Do all the good you
can, by all the means you
can, in all the ways you
can, at all the times you
can, to all the people you
can, as long as you
ever can.

John Wesley

What is moral is what you feel good after and what is immoral is what you feel bad after.

Ernest Hemingway

If all men were basically evil, who would bother to improve the world instead of giving it up as a bad job at the outset?

Van Wyck Brooks

There is nothing evil save that which perverts the mind and shackles the conscience.

St. Ambrose

Evil often triumphs, but never conquers.

Joseph Roux

Everything in the universe has a purpose. Indeed, the invisible intelligence that flows through everything in a purposeful fashion is also flowing through you.

Dr. Waye Dyer

Act as if every event has a purpose, and your life will have purpose.

Andrew Matthews

Learn to get in touch with the silence within yourself and know that everything in this life has a purpose.

Elisabeth Kübler Ross

You create your reality with your intentions.

Gary Zukav

At each moment you choose the intentions that will shape your experiences and those things upon which you will focus your attention. If you choose, you evolve consciously.

Gary Zukav

The nearest way to glory is to strive to be what you wish to be, thought to be.

Socrates

If any man seeks for greatness, let him forget greatness and ask for truth, and he will find both.

H. Mann

Knowledge and courage take turns at greatness.

Baltasar Gracian

The deepest secret is that life is not a process of discovery, but a process of creation. You are not discovering yourself, but creating yourself anew. Seek, therefore, not to find out who you are, seek to determine who you want to be.

Neale Donald Walsch

Knowledge comes,

but wisdom lingers.

Tennyson

It is easier to be wise for others than for ourselves.

La Rochefoucauld

The thoughtful soul
to solitude retires.

Rubaiyat of Omar Khayyam

Loneliness can be conquered only by those who can bear solitude.

Paul Tilch

I never found the companion that was so companionable as solitude.

Thoreau

I regret often that I have spoken, never that I have been quiet.

Syrus

Without silence there is no music; there is only noise.

M. Scott Peck

Members who speak not a word may contribute as much to a group as the most voluble.

M. Scott Peck

The process of prayer becomes much easier when, rather than having to believe that God will always say yes to every request, one understands intuitively that the request itself is not necessary.

Neale Donald Walsch

A prayer, in its simplest definition, is merely a wish turned heavenward.

P. Brooks

Prayer is the voice of faith.

Horne

No prayer — and a prayer is nothing more than a fervent statement of what is so — goes unanswered.

Neale Donald Walsch

Intuition is the voice of the nonphysical world.

Gary Zukav

Intuition is the spiritual faculty that does not explain, it simply points the way.

Florence Scoval Schinn

Intuition is really a sudden immersion of the soul into the universal current of life, where the histories of all people are connected, and we are able to know everything, because it's all written there.

Paulo Coelho

It is not God's
function to create or
uncreate the circumstances
and conditions of your life.
God created You, in the
image and likeness of God.
You have created the rest.

Neale Donald Walsch

Living in process is being open to insight and encounter. Creativity is becoming intensively absorbed in the process and giving it form.

Susan Smith

You are in the process of experiencing yourself by creating yourself anew in every single moment. As I am. Through you.

Neale Donald Walsch

Everything that we experience, everything we think, feel and do is in divine order. It is part of the universal flow that helps us discover who we are. If our thoughts and emotions did not manifest as actions, how else would we see who we are? The world is not happening to us. We are happening to it.

Anon

There is no separation between us and God; we are divine expressions of the creative principle on this level of existence.

Shakti Gawain

Our humanity were a
poor thing but for the
divinity that stirs
within us.

Francis Bacon

I can have a self or I can have consistent behaviour. I cannot have both.

Hugh Prather

It is in the giving up of the self that human beings can find the most ecstatic and lasting, solid, durable joy of life.

M. Scott Peck

It is through hearing — and obeying — the demand to make a life adjustment that the ability to face oneself grows. In fact, many abilities grow along with self-trust.... As each correction is made, the bond between self and Self grows stronger, thus giving more power to the voice of Self, more clarity and purpose to the individual life.

Marsha Sinetar

Self is the only prison that can ever bind the soul.

Henry Van Dyke

Don't fight a fact, deal with it. Don't discard your self, be more of it.

Hugh Prather

The most sacred place isn't the Church, the Mosque or the Temple. It's the temple of the body. That's where the spirit lives.

Susan Taylor

The one thing grander than the sea is the sky. The one thing greater than the sky is the spirit of the human being.

Anon

One truth stands firm. All that happens in the world history rests on something spiritual. If the spiritual is strong, it creates world history. If it is weak, it suffers world history.

A. Schweitzer

Spirit is slippery. It does not submit itself to definition, to capture, the way material things do.

M. Scott Peck

You are not a human being having a spiritual experience. You are a spiritual being having a human experience.

Dr. Wayne Dyer

We are not born all at once, but by bits. The body first, and the spirit later.

Mary Antin

The human spirit is stronger than anything that happens to it.

C. C. Scott

Nothing can dim the light which shines from within.

Maya Angelou

Nature never repeats herself and the possibilities of one human soul will never be found in another.

Elizabeth Cady Stanton

The work of the soul is to wake yourself up. The work of God is to wake everybody else up.

Neale Donald Walsch

Everyone should know that you can't live in any other way than by cultivating the soul.

Thomas Moore

Our echoes roll from soul to soul, and grow forever and ever.

Tennyson

The one thing in the world of value, is the active soul.

Emerson

Signs from the soul come silently, as silently as the sun enters the world.

A Tibetan saying

When you hold the breath, you hold the soul.

B. K. S. Iyengar

The soul leads you to the right and perfect opportunities for you to experience exactly what you had planned to experience. What you actually experience is up to you.

Neale Donald Walsch

The soul should always stand ajar, ready to welcome the ecstatic experience.

Emily Dickinson

While everyone has a different experience of what is soulful, these experiences do share similar beginnings. We start by giving ourselves permission to be soulful, to take seriously this aspect of ourselves, our soul and our soul's need.

Jean Shinoda Bolen

When your life is filled with the desire to see the holiness in everyday life, something magical happens: ordinary life becomes extraordinary, and the very process of life begins to nourish your soul.

Rabbi Harold Kushner

The soul — your soul — knows all there is to know all the time. There is nothing hidden to it, nothing unknown. Yet knowing is not enough. The soul seeks to experience.

Neale Donald Walsch

The soul is here for its own joy.

Rumi

There is in this world no such force as the force of a man determined to rise. The human soul cannot be permanently chained.

W. E. B. DuBois

Allow each soul to walk its path.

Neale Donald Walsch

Heaven is where you'll be when you are okay right where you are.

Sun Ra

Seek not outside yourself, heaven is within.

Mary Lou Cook

When it is time to die,
let us not discover that
we never lived.

Henry David Thoreau

One must wait until evening to see how splendid the day was; one cannot judge life until death.

Charles de Gaulle

No one who is fit to live need fear to die.... To us here, death is the most terrible word we know. But when we have tasted its reality, it will mean to us birth, deliverance, a new creation of ourselves.

G. S. Merriam

My God, this is a hell of a job. I have no trouble with my enemies. I can take care of my enemies all right. But my damn friends, my goddamn friends. They're the ones that keep me walking the floor nights.

Warren G. Harding

There is no such thing as death,
In nature, nothing dies:
From each sad moment of decay
Some forms of life arise.

Charles Mackay

It is by dying that one awakens to eternal life.

Anon

It is death that provides life with all its meaning.

M. Scott Peck

A rose given during life is better than orchids on the grave.

Anon

The bitterest tears shed over graves are for words left unsaid and deeds left undone.

Harriet Beecher Stowe

A smile is a curve that sets everything straight.

Phyllis Diller